This Book belongs to

Abbie Brown

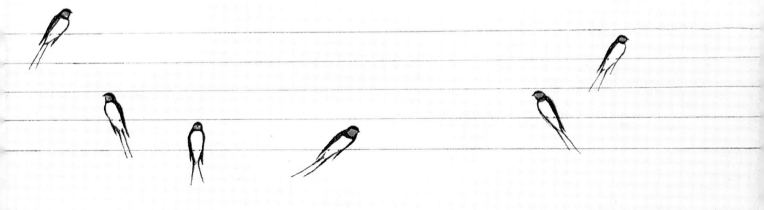

TO MY YOUNGEST SON

SINGING RASCALS DO
Original Finnish title LAULUVIIKARIN DO

This series of books is based on the teaching method developed by
Géza Szilvay and is part of the instructional material
used by the Colourstrings Music Kindergartens.

The melodies in the SINGING RASCALS series reappear in the colourstrings/
colourkeys instrumental beginners books. Pupils find this
very helpful during the early stages of learning an instrument.

For further details of
Colourstrings Music Kindergartens
write to the publishers:

COLOURSTRINGS INTERNATIONAL LIMITED
26 MEADOW LANE
SUDBURY, SUFFOLK
ENGLAND, CO10 2TD

Printers: Ebenezer Baylis & Son Ltd, Worcester, and London

ISBN 1-873604-14-9
ISMN M-708023-07-4

SINGING RASCALS

DO

Géza Szilvay

Illustrations:
Tuulia Hyrske

Words:
Angela Ailes

SONGS:

COLOURSTRINGS INTERNATIONAL LIMITED
SUDBURY, SUFFOLK

DASHING DAN

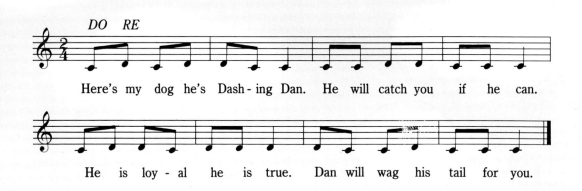

Here's my dog he's Dash-ing Dan. He will catch you if he can.

He is loy - al he is true. Dan will wag his tail for you.

RE
DO

MY DOLLY MOLLY

MI   RE   DO

This is lit - tle Mol - ly, Mol - ly is my dol - ly.

Doc - tor can you mend her leg? Do it gent - ly please I beg.

Now Mol - ly please try, do be brave and don't cry.

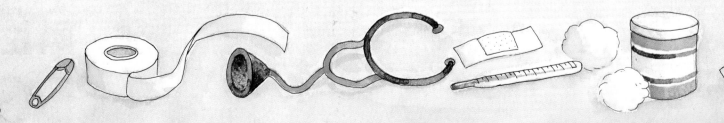

MI
RE
DO

LITTLE TRAIN

DO RE MI

Choo choo choo choo choo choo choo choo, 'Hur - ry lit - tle puff - er train,'

FA

Cried all the child - ren, See our mer - ry flags are wav - ing to and fro,

Now when the sta - tion mas - ter blows his shi - ny whis - tle, Toot toot toot toot off we'll go.

FA
MI
RE
DO

ELSIE THE ELEPHANT

DO   *RE*   *MI*

El - sie is an el - e - phant who wants to play. She is

SO

mus - ic - al and big and grey. She is good at sing - ing Mi Re

FA

Do. That's why the lit - tle child - ren love her so.

SO
FA
MI
RE
DO

COWBOY JOE

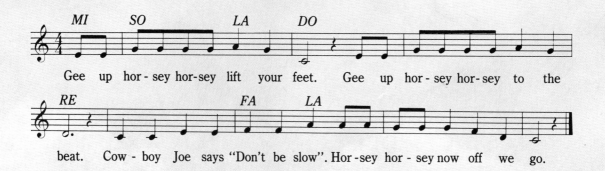

Gee up hor - sey hor-sey lift your feet. Gee up hor-sey hor-sey to the beat. Cow - boy Joe says "Don't be slow". Hor -sey hor - sey now off we go.

LA
SO
FA
MI
RE
DO

MOUSEY

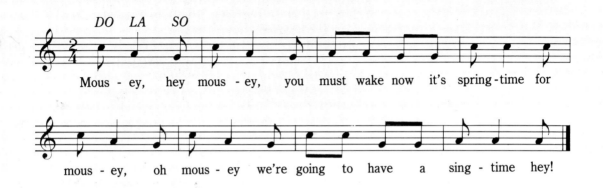

Mous - ey, hey mous - ey, you must wake now it's spring - time for

mous - ey, oh mous - ey we're going to have a sing - time hey!

DO
LA
SO

CHUCK CHUCK CHICKENS

Chuck chuck chick-ens slee - py heads, now it is time to leave your beds.

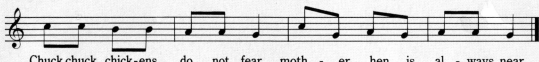

Chuck chuck chick-ens do not fear, moth - er hen is al - ways near.

16

DO TI
LA
SO

INCY WINCY SPIDER

DO RE MI

In - cy win - cy spi - der climbed up the spout.

FA SO

Down came the rain and washed the spi - der out.

DO TI LA

Out came the sun - shine, dried up all the rain.

In - cy win - cy spi - der climbed the spout a - gain.

DO
TI
LA
SO
FA
MI
RE
DO

DO

RE

MI

FA

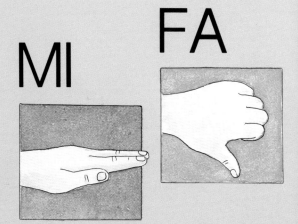

SO

LA

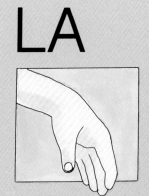

TI

DO

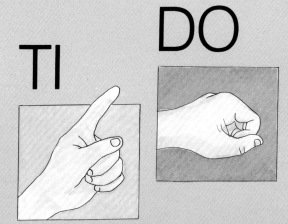

MESSAGE FROM DR. GÉZA SZILVAY
Head of the East Helsinki Music Institute and compiler of the
"Singing Rascals" series

Many children today have all the material things they need: clothes, food, toys, etc; sometimes they have more than enough. Material things, however, cannot replace the warmth affection and time we give to the child, which is so important for its spiritual nourishment.

The "Singing Rascals" books are intended as a means of helping parents, grandparents, kindergarten and nursery school teachers, and all those who have children in their care, to create stimulating and purposeful moments with them.

The pictures, melodies, and words in these books have been carefully chosen and arranged with young pre-school children in mind. The tunes have been selected from those which over the years have proved appealing and easy to learn, and are skilfully illustrated. The characters may be used to make up tales arising from the songs. The printed notation is only for the use of the adults.

The songs progress from two notes up to five notes (pentatonic) or seven notes (diatonic). Although for the sake of clarity they are written in C major and A minor, singing them in different keys, i.e. from different starting notes, is to be encouraged, thus suiting the children's own pitch registers. The use of solfa marking (Do-Re) makes it easy for parents to learn basic solmisation while the children enjoy learning the pitch names and hand signs.

The series is supported by a parallel series of audio tapes on which infants sing and young children perform the melodies, but no cassette, however good, can replace the lap and guidance of the close relative or friend.

The creation of Colourstrings Music Kindergartens is a significant step forward in the music education of the very young, and one in which I feel proud to play a part. My wish for all the little members is – joyous singing!

Géza Szilvay

Composers:

Dashing Dan
Jorma Ollaranta.

My Dolly Molly
*

The Little Train
*

Elsie the Elephant
*

Cowboy Joe
*

Mousey
Zoltán Kodály

Chuck Chuck Chickens
*

Incy Wincy Spider
*

*Tunes based on children's and folk melodies.